The 18 Laws of Employer Branding

James Ellis

Legal TL;DR:
It's mine, so I'll do what I want with it.
What I want is for you to take as much of it as you need.
Share it. Use it. Copy it. Attribute it.

Table of Contents

Introduction
Law #1: The Law of Strategy
Law #2: The Law of Focus
Law #3: The Law of Perception
Law #4: The Law of Provenance
Law #5: The Law of Impact
Law #6: The Law of Desire
Law #7: The Law of Quality
Law #8: The Law of Fit
Law #9: The Law of Clarity
Law #10: The Law of Subjectivity
Law #11: The Law of Localization
Law #12: The Law of Activation
Law #13: The Law of Options
Law #14: The Law of Customers
Law #15: The Law of Expansion
Law #16: The Law of Relationships
Law #17: The Law of Humanity
Law #18: The Law of One Brand
Conclusion
Also by James Ellis

Introduction

Employer brand has been "a thing" for more than 30 years.

According to LinkedIn (apply your own "grain of salt" rule here), there are 34,000 people who call themselves an employer brander, and 600,000 more who list employer branding as a skill.

There are dozens of agencies in the US alone who specialize in employer branding.

So why does it feel like we're all still fumbling around in the dark looking for a light switch?

Now, I have no issue with the idea that there are a million ways to do good employer branding, but without some kind of shared sense of "the basics," it feels like each new generation of branders figure things out just in time to move onto their next function and fail to pass things down.

Heck, in some employer brand forum right now, there is someone with the title of "employer brand manager" asking, "how do you build an employer brand?" You don't see recruiters asking, "hey, I just got this job: how do I recruit?"

So let's set up some basic laws that you can apply to your employer branding, regardless of your approach.

Hence, the laws of employer branding.

Enjoy!

-James

P.S. This book was written without the help of AI or ChatGPT. Is it weird that I feel the need to say that?

-J

Law #1: The Law of Strategy

Employer brand is strategy, not tactics (though you'll still need tactics)

For a very long time, when it came to warfare, the largest army won. It was simple math: each soldier was about as effective as any other, so having more meant you would win.

Every once in a while, someone would defy the odds. Rather than array their people in the "typical" way, they would try something different. Maybe they would put their weakest people in the front instead of the strongest. Maybe they would employ trickery to make it seem like they had more people than they did. Maybe it was a feint to the right and a strong attack to the left.

Sometimes it was as simple as choosing the battleground, like when the 300 Spartans faced off against thousands by forcing the far larger army through a mountain pass, negating the army's strength and making the battle more of a one-on-one affair.

This is strategy: Making decisions about how to use your resources to achieve maximum impact. Whether it's against an opponent across the battlefield or the dozens of companies against whom you compete for talent, you can (and should) make choices about how, who, when and where you fight.

But classic recruiting feels a lot more like medieval warfare, where one army (of mostly farmers and serfs) holding swords and pikes fought against another army (again, mostly of farmers and serfs) with similar tools. Line 'em up, let 'em rip. We look at recruiters in a similar vein: few are "trained" in recruiting and they have the same databases and outreach tools as every other recruiter in every other company. We line 'em up and let 'em rip.

It seems strange to think that we've optimized around this idea, that recruiting teams get better when they get bigger, or get "the latest tools." And so TA leaders fight their fight in terms of headcount and budget.

Employer branding, at its core, is strategy: Who do we want to hire? Why do we want them? What do we offer? Why would they want that? What will they get out of working here? Who is looking for the stuff we offer? Where are they now and what do they get now? How are we different from other companies? Where do they look for information about jobs? How do we talk to people outside the funnel versus thus within it? What policies and news can we leverage to tell our story in a more credible way?

This isn't letting 'em rip. This is thinking about the creation of an advantage without more resources. This is about maximizing existing resources, sometimes by making the individual recruiter more effective, sometimes by seeing a bigger picture and creating resources from outside TA, and sometimes by defining and building a position that just makes the company more attractive.

Employer branding works best when it starts with that strategy and builds tactics and plans that execute on the strategy. Sure, employer branding is building LinkedIn posts (tactic) and writing better job postings (tactic) and implementing a better referral program (tactics) and implementing your first CRM (tactic) and training hiring managers to use the brand talking points to attract great talent (tactic) etc. But those tactics without a strategy are noise, like your favorite book with the chapters put in random order. The words and sentences are the same, but the book is confusing rather than enthralling.

Why this works

Recruiters are tasked with requisitions. They do the crucial retail work of translating hiring manager desires to the marketplace. They source, engage, attract, persuade, build relationships and shepherd great people who will make the business run. As such, they often feel the effects of a lack of strategy (we're going up against the biggest companies and we aren't interesting enough, we're going against other companies and sound just like them, no one knows who we are, no one has a reason to open my outreach emails, I think the career site is three years out of date, etc) and sometimes they can diagnose the lack of strategy (who's in charge of making sure we're known in the market? Is there any central support for this tool or is it every recruiter for themselves? etc), but they are too busy swimming to build a boat.

At the same time TA leadership is busy playing defense, protecting the TA team from hiring manager frustrations while translating TA frustrations into potential new resources. And HR focuses on creating an equitable process for all, not helping the company stand out in a crowded talent marketplace.

And marketing is (rightly) focused on more leads not better leads, which is anathema to recruiting, who only can put one person into a given role. And broadly, strategic thinking about the consumer market is often (and perhaps correctly) seen as more valuable than imperfect strategy about the talent market.

This leaves a gap for employer branding to own. To see the bigger picture, to create deeper relationships across the company, to look at the talent market as a whole and define an interesting position within it, to build the content and marketing that defends that position. That is where employer branding lives.

Where this falls apart

As employer branding is a young field, it is often staffed with less experienced marketers or recruiters (there is no training ground for employer branding skill other than being a junior employer brander). Leadership often looks skeptically at a 26-year-old trying to develop strategy for a function that requires 4-7% of its entire operating budget. So the employer brander is reduced to a tactical role. That employer brander will be tasked with "pretty words, pretty pictures" rather than the strategic work that will yield the most benefit.

Examples

In 1999, a company almost no one heard of in Cary, North Carolina made the cover of Fast Company because it offered what seemed like an insane amount of perks and benefits to its staff. Among other things, SAS offered meals, snacks, child care, health care and a workout facility on site for free. Because they took care of their people, word spread and the people who liked that much support would all but fall over each other to apply. A strategy of abundant benefits lead to hiring great talent at a far lower recruiting cost. Could they have offered less perks and saved a little money? Sure. Would the company make the cover of a national magazine about how amazing they were? No. Their strategy was to be better at one thing than anyone else, which effectively created its own gravitational pull for talent.

By hiring entry level talent almost exclusively, Enterprise Holdings can hire en masse at a very low cost. That budget is poured into its training and development teams to take great raw materials and turn them into amazing managers, salespeople and workers. Theirs is a strategy of "build, don't buy."

So what is your talent strategy? How will you array your resources to create maximum impact?

Law #2: The Law of Focus

Brands are decision-making filters, both on the candidate side but also on the company side

What's the difference between Coke and Pepsi? Or Nike and Adidas? Or Ford and Toyota? Or Kate Spade and Coach?

These choices, removed from their brand associations, aren't really choices. The difference between Coke and Pepsi boils down to one being slightly sweeter than the other, but not in an obvious way. The difference between Ford and Toyota mostly boils down to which side of the car the fuel tank lives. Can you say for certain that the Kate Spade bag and the Coach bag were not made in the same factory by the same people?

Branding originated as the world moved from local agrarian economies where you knew the blacksmith and the barrel maker and the guy who sold you a horse (whatever one calls that job). You may have known these people your entire life, as you and they grew up rarely moving more than a few miles away from your birthplaces. This meant, you knew their parents and you knew their kids. So if they sold you a bad horseshoe or a sick horse to put it on, it was in everyone's best interests to find a solution. If the blacksmith didn't make it right, the entire town would know in a heartbeat. Their reputation would be destroyed. Thus, they were incentivized to create quality goods.

As the industrial revolution moved through, suddenly you didn't know the man who made your barrel. In fact, it was a team of nameless unknown folks in a factory who built it. So since you no longer have any connection to the people who built a thing, how do you know it will be good?

By applying a brand to their work, the company was saying, "If you bought this before and liked it, you'll like this, too." The brand was their reputation.

But as brands became prominent, brands were not just indications of quality, but an indication of perspective. Buy my horse if you want the best and are willing to spend a little more, buy their horse if you don't need a top-of-the-line horse. The brand indicated for whom the products were built.

Brands became filters. If you were the sort to keep up with fashion, buy their shirt. If you don't believe in unnecessary decoration, buy my shirt. If you support the monarchy, read this newspaper, but if you support a more democratic regime, read ours. You choose the brand that best fits you and ignore the brands that don't align with your needs and beliefs.

In employer branding, this means communicating who you are for. Are you for the salesperson who likes to work autonomously or the one who likes to collaborate as part of a team? Are you for the recruiter who prefers a high salary and small bonus or the one who wants a smaller salary and a much larger potential bonus? Are you for the developer who has to work on the latest and greatest, or the developer that likes working in an environment where you are encouraged to do thoughtful, elegant work?

Some people would rather work at Patagonia than Koch because of their beliefs. Some chose Tesla and Twitter for its leadership, while others avoid it for the same reason.

Your brand is a filter to candidates: this is the reason you choose us or don't choose us.

That filter works in both directions. As it provides a reason for people to filter the company in or out of their consideration set, it also filters people into or out of the company.

+++++

You can use any tool or tactic to attempt to talk to pretty much anyone. The internet has broken down the barriers and gatekeepers to people, expanding our reach to the near-infinite. But just because you can reach someone doesn't mean your message will be valued (or responded to) by that person. There will always be people who want to hear what you have to say more than others.

Thinking about your brand as a filter demands that you create focus. Focus of what you value, focus of what you think about, focus of what kind of person is going to be successful, focus of who you are and who you aren't.

Who do you want and who don't you want? What does your target audience care about that your non-target audience does not?

Seth Godin says the core of a brand is, "People like us do things like this." If you are like us, make these choices. And these choices signal that you're part of our group. Those choices are specific, subtle, imbued with a secret meaning only the tribe members understand.

This is the power of focus: The more you focus, the better you get at the thing you focus on and the more clear you are to your audience, the more believable you are, and the cheaper it is to support that message.

Why this works

As you create more of a focus on the kinds of people you want to hire (by temperament, skill set, location, ambition, motivation, etc), you will become better at communicating that idea. Talk about the ins and outs of modern nursing every day for three months and you will realize you're peeling the onion of a nurse's work experience. You're getting past the obvious platitudes into the stuff only nurses say to each other.

You aren't talking to "health care professional types," but "nurses working in small hospitals in North Florida." You aren't talking to "new nurses," but the "nurses who just graduated from Loyola in the middle of their class: the kind who didn't get great grades because nursing wasn't something that just made sense, but a craft, something that needed to be worked at every day."

Think of how the greatest writers write. A Farewell To Arms starts, "In the late summer of that year we lived in a house in a village that looked across the river and the plain to the mountains. In the bed of the river there were pebbles and boulders, dry and white in the sun, and the water was clear and swiftly moving and blue in the channels." Not, "It was pretty hot that summer we lived near a river." The first paints a picture in specifics. The second conveys only broad strokes.

The more you write, the deeper you dig towards something more meaningful. Something more real. You write your way into their world, creating an audience that sees you not as an interloper looking to sell something, but as a member of the community. This creates credibility you cannot buy.

Where this falls apart

The value and power of the filter only come into play when the brand is clear on who or what it wants to filter in and who or what it wants to filter out. Arbitrary focus isn't useful. It starts when you truly understand what your company is all about, the attributes and behaviors it rewards, and who it simply isn't built for.

Examples

The Ritz-Carlton hotel has one of my favorite employer brand/consumer marketing messages: We are ladies and gentlemen serving ladies and gentlemen. They aren't looking to hire "experienced hospitality staff" or "maids with a can-do attitude" or "housekeepers with 3-5 years experience." They know who they are, why they are, and how they are. They are drawing a very clear line between people who would be good fits and people who would not, all in one line.

Law #3: The Law of Perception

Your employer brand only exists in someone else's head

I often catch myself deploying seemingly endless metaphors when I teach people about branding. It's a filter. It's cement blocks we drop in the ocean. It's what people say about us. It's an emotional connection. It's a living organism. A brand is context. Or it's the personification of the organization.

Look, I love metaphors 6.4 times more than most people, but this seems excessive. We all know what a brand is, right? We've been surrounded by them our entire lives. They influence us in big ways and small. Heck, we make a living by building and using them.

In a way, asking anyone in the modern world what a brand is, is a lot like asking a fish what water is. We're surrounded and inundated by it, that we often lose sight of what it is.

Because, when you pull the layers back, you start to realize that a brand isn't... anything.

It isn't something you can see. It isn't something you can touch. For all the time, money, and energy we put into our brands, they aren't really ours.

"Your" brand exists solely in other people's heads. While it can be influenced and nudged, that brand is 100% how others perceive your company, your products, and what it's like to work there.

This law is very much a double-edged sword. First because as something that isn't "real" in any sense of the word, we cannot directly affect it.

So how can you be responsible for the brand if you have no direct impact on it? Through influence.

If we add another metaphor to the mix, the brand is like a bird's nest. When building a nest, the bird picks up what it can where it can. Whatever it finds becomes the nest. In a city, a bird next might have coffee stirrers and bits of receipts. In a forest, it will be made of pine needles and twigs. In an open area, it will be made of grass and straw. The only way you can change a bird's nest is to change what materials are available and accessible to it.

Like a bird collecting material for a nest, your brand is made up of all sorts of experiences and touchpoints the person had with your brand. You can't change how someone sees your brand, but you can surround them with new messages and proof points. With intention, you can seed the ground with the things you want to become the nest. You can't get into the nest and make it into something new (if you do, the bird will never enter it again because it is no longer the bird's), all you can do is make it easy for the bird to build the nest you want it to make.

That means, changing brand perception can take time. But the good news is that once set, it can take a lot of time to change it again.

But because it isn't "real" it allows us to expand the parameters of the game in a way that gives us almost infinite options on how to approach our world. Options that extend way beyond the logo and website.

Would changing the script that customer service uses influence people's perception of the brand? Yes.

Would changing the outgoing voicemail message change people's perception? Yes. (And I know someone who became interested in a company specifically because of that outgoing message, so try and fight me.)

Would making sure every interviewee gets a box of cookies delivered to their home change perception? Oh yes.

None of these things are classically seen as something that employer branding needs to worry about, but when you see that the name of the game is perception influence, you can find so many ways to influence that perception.

Why this works

As we talked about in the Law of Focus, brands were ways to indicate who made something because we became more and more disconnected from the maker of the thing. They started as a kind of reputation mark, a way of indicating that someone who made your last great shirt made this shirt, too.

But what makes a great shirt? Or horseshoe? Or bag of flour? Quality is completely subjective. What makes a great shirt to one isn't important to someone else. Thus, the brand extends beyond reputation and into perception.

Where this falls apart

No less an "authority" than the American Marketing Association defines a brand in terms of its physical and visual assets. Your logo, your colors, your imagery, your fonts, your style, etc. Sorry, but that isn't a brand. Some might refer to it as "branding" but it is a visual identity, not a brand.

For example, Nike's swoosh is likely one of the world's best-known logos. And when some people see it, they think of athleticism, physical achievement, and the glory of winning. And when others see it, they see an over-priced, over-marketed set of shoes. Same logo, but very different brand perspectives.

I bring this up because many people who don't really "do" branding make this false equivalency all the time. They assume an employer brand is your style of writing more than the choice of what to write about. They think the hashtag counts for more than the content it gets attached to. They might make a variation of the logo for you, but ignore what that logo is now supposed to stand for.

Don't fall into this trap. The brand exists in a stranger's mind, a place you can't touch directly.

Examples

There was a time when Old Spice was the aftershave your granddad wore. It was a brand signifying a kind of old-school rugged man, possibly a fisherman, who slapped someone to try and get rid of the aroma of yesterday's catch of the day.

Today, Old Spice has roughly the same logo, color scheme and typography as its sea-faring ancestor, but it isn't old school anymore. Whether it's the now classic "the man your man could smell like" campaign or the current "smelf-confidence" [sic] ads, this is a brand for far younger men. Without changing much of the core brand identity, the company has changed what the brand stands for and how you likely think about it.

How? By changing everything around the brand. The commercials. The scents. The target audience. The product selection (Old Spice makes way more from deodorants and soaps than it does from aftershave). The language around the product family. They changed people's perceptions by surrounding them with changed information and values.

Law #4: The Law of Provenance

The employer brand comes from every single part of the company (and informs each part in turn)

Everything the company does IS the brand.

This is good and bad news.

The good news is that you have the chance to work with literally ANYONE within the company and be able to make an impact. From the executive assistant who decides what the outgoing voicemail message should be to the internal comms manager who is scripting the all-hands meeting, to the customer service manager who is adjusting language used by call centers, to the marketers and developers who manage the corporate website, to the IT team who decides the default wallpaper on all computers assigned to staff and what ends up on the digital signage, etc etc etc.

You can do good work from literally any part of the company.

The bad news is that the company is huge compared to you, and every single element of the company may call on you at any time for advice, copy, images, strategies, video, and event support (and who knows what else). You are a single person with a straw, stepping up to the ocean to drink it dry.

You are more likely to grow wings than you are to complete 20% of the good ideas you have in that list you keep on your phone of things you think might be fun, or cool, or useful or helpful.

Without opening up the can of worms marked, "Where should the employer brand function live?" this law simply embraces that no matter where the function lives, its scope is far wider than its spot in the organization chart.

Compared to a consumer brand, where perception is localized to the product, its availability, and the service around it, there are seemingly infinite cooks putting their hands in an employer brand's pot.

That's why only crazy people do this job: you are expected to be responsible for the output of every aspect of the company, but have zero authority to make changes to that output.

The Law of Provenance spawns two crucial corollaries: The Rule Of Influence and the Rule of Authenticity.

The Rule of Influence states that as you have no authority over all the teams who are saying, shipping and publishing things that change people's perception of your brand, you need to spend a lot of your time building relationships with all those people. You need to help them understand the impact of customer service, feature development, ESG, PR, and recruiting (among many many others) have on the brand, and (more directly) their own ability to hire.

The Rule of Authenticity states that since branding messages are coming from every part of the company, the most effective way to align messages around the brand is to ensure the brand makes sense to everyone and reflects the organization's approach to... whatever it is they do. The value in authenticity isn't moral. The value is in its effectiveness, that people are going to do what they have always been doing, it is easier to wrap those actions in a brand idea than it is to get dozens of teams to change.

Why this works

According to the Law of Perception, the brand we seek to influence lives in other people's heads, and is ultimately a construct of accumulated experiences, touchpoints and interactions with the company.

Thus, all elements of the company are nudging the employer brand in various directions. What the recruiter says in the outreach email and how much customer service seems to care about their customer's problems have equal weight and impact on the brand.

Instead of thinking about a company as a series of semi-related functions, see it as a large organism, where attributes from one part impact the attributes from others. Imagine a giraffe or a deer with one leg shorter than the rest. That short shapes how well the animal can run, regardless of how strong the other three are.

When you are looking at an employer brand, you're looking at the sum of an entire organization, even if the responsibility of the employer brand falls to talent acquisition, comms or marketing. What someone on the other side of the company does can have just as big an influence on what the public sees and feels about the company as thousands of dollars in ad budget and the planning of a dozen people.

Where this falls apart

The obvious challenge with this law is that no matter how often you explain that every part of the company is shaping the brand, companies prefer to know exactly who can be blamed for problems. They are going to make one person or team responsible for the brand so that they have a single "throat to choke" so to speak.

No matter how diligent or organized, no matter how prescient, you will not be able to know everything a company is doing. The law means that part of your time managing the brand is going to go toward building space and slack in the system, giving yourself room to adjust and react to messes you can't anticipate.

This need to build in space and gaps will seem like a drag on your productivity, but as you are regularly interrupted by crises well beyond your scope and expected to react to them, that space will keep you from having to throw your more strategic projects by the wayside.

Examples

There are ample examples of companies making big claims about their employer brand, their cultures and their values to candidates, but not living those examples within the rest of the company.

We can start with companies who fly pride flags all over their careers page in June to show how inclusive they are, but then donate to politicians actively seeking to limit the rights of people in the LGBTQ+ community. When the company is talking out of both sides of its mouth, who is a candidate supposed to believe? The marketer or the executive cutting the check?

Of course, we have the companies who talk about how much they care about valuing women in the workspace but only offer the legal minimum of family leave. It doesn't matter how many women are in the hero image on the career site if allowances aren't made for the women and their families.

Or the companies who talk about their dedication to innovative approaches, but ask you to retype your resume into the ATS after you've uploaded it. Sure, the company didn't code the ATS, but they made the choice to be okay with outdated technology for candidates because... well because those people aren't important to the company yet.

These examples are almost always negative: the company plays up how much it lives by its values as a marketing tactic, but then chooses to throw those values out the moment it becomes complex, painful, expensive, or politically expedient. So I won't name names, but I suspect I won't have to. We all know companies paint over the cracks (and worse) of the foundation with a coat of glossy paint.

That might work in consumer marketing, but in employer branding, the cracks always come through.

Law #5: The Law of Impact

Employer brand impacts every part of the company

Let's get something clear from the jump. People are not your company's greatest asset. People are your company. Full stop.

Without people, a company is a taxation number and a set of legal rules. The entire purpose of a company is to enable a group of people to do more together than an individual could do. By itself, it does nothing. It makes nothing. In pretty much every sense, a company without people is nothing.

This means that for all the value that marketing brings to the table to get people to understand why people should buy a product or like a brand, employer branding owns the human side of the brand.

This is of note because it turns out that companies are just people.

People who work in development. People who work in sales. People who work in HR. People who work in procurement. People who work in marketing. People who work in operations. They all need to hire people, which means, they need to have a compelling message around their differentiated value that they can share to attract and hire the people who will grow that team and the company as a whole.

Pro tip: Having issues with a certain team? (*cough*marketing*cough*) Wait until they have a critical role that isn't filling fast enough (spoiler: it is NEVER filling fast enough) and then offer to help. When they see how you work, and how what you do is different from how they work, they will start to see your value more and ask you to show up to more meetings.

But the employer brand impacts the entire company because the company's people are the driver for every choice and decision made at the company. That new feature the press is raving about? People did that. That customer service that people are complaining about? People made the decisions as to what constitutes "good service." That account manager who went above and beyond to save the account? That person probably worked with other people to solve the problem. The executive being sued for creating a toxic work environment? Despite all evidence, that is actually a person.

So if people are the lifeblood of a company, there is value in having everyone who works there understand the shared goals, mission, values and behaviors of the company. People aligned towards the same ideas generally have higher productivity.

Conversely, everyone knows the stories of companies that let the one over-performing jerk get away with things because they bring in so much business, but in the end that tolerated behavior poisons the well for everyone else. The one person (and the leadership who refuses to fix the problem) reshapes the culture negatively.

Alignment here creates its own value. When people have a shared understanding of the "rules" of working at the company, when they all see the same goalposts, they work better. They work with less rancor. They have less friction, and any existing friction is resolved faster and more amicably.

Why this works

The employer brand defines and describes to people on the outside how the company works and what it rewards. It sets the frame around which people set their expectations about what the experience will be like and the likelihood that they will be satisfied.

The power of this becomes obvious when you see it through the flywheel. Let's say you offer autonomy to candidates. Candidates who want and value autonomy are more likely to apply and get hired, thus increasing the number of people at work who value autonomy, which in turn attracts more people who value autonomy. The employer brand creates its own self-fulfilling prophecy because it is the thinking around the impression a company makes to a candidate.

Where this falls apart

One of the core frictions in our work is balancing what we see and hear from staff every day and the company that leadership thinks it is (or wants it to be). So when the brand is emanating from every part of the company and impacting every part of the company, a lack of alignment with what leadership intentions and aspirations becomes obvious. The net result is a fragmented sense of what it's like to work there, thereby hamstringing the brand's ability to help the company.

The other major obstacle here is the company's unwillingness to see how the brand, which encapsulates the work experience, values and culture (among other things) being the kind of "operating instructions" for working at the company. Many teams see themselves as special or independent of what "the rest of the company" thinks (see developers in the early days of Facebook or traders in an investment firm).

Examples

For companies where the people are the most obviously differentiating value, this law is crystal clear. Think of an airline. Every airline has to fly through the same cities and airports. Every airline has to cover the same geography through the same airspace. They all fly the same planes. The biggest difference between a Delta and a United are the people who work there: the people staffing the gate handling onboardings and delays, the flight attendants providing service, the baggage handlers making sure your luggage gets where it needs to go in one piece, and the pilots being committed to safety and speed.

In companies like these, it doesn't take much at all to see the difference between a strong and clear brand and one which is all "pretty words and pictures" with nothing underpinning it.

This is also true for consulting firms, where a McKinsey or EY might have an operating philosophy or process, but in the end, it's the people who create connections, build solutions and serve the customer. Where it pretty much doesn't matter who is staffing the grill at McDonald's, the output is meant to be fool-proof and the same whether you're eating in Hoboken or Hollywood, your only interaction with a consultant firm comes through the consultant assigned to the project. Thus, the brand has an outsized impact on who is attracted to the company and how the firm is ultimately seen by customers.

Law #6: The Law of Desire

Talent has to choose you first, so you need to be on their "list" before they start looking

Let's play a game. I'll make up a company (FakeCorp) and spend $10,000 posting fake job postings to job boards.

Now, there is no company of this name, so you won't be surprised to learn that there's no career site, LinkedIn channel, Glassdoor reviews, videos on YouTube, or anything at all beyond the job post (that quite clearly says, "sponsored" next to it).

So with all that in mind, I have a question: Do you expect to get a quality applicant out of this?

$10,000 isn't a small amount of money. For many companies, it is their complete annual recruiting ad budget. For that kind of spend (according to vendors), you should expect good candidates to apply.

But is that what you expect will happen?

Me neither.

Instead, you'll get a pile of resumes of people who mostly didn't even read the fake job posting. They will be people who don't come close to meeting the most basic qualifications. (I'm not talking "if it offers six requirements and you only meet five, apply anyway" way of thinking, but more in an "in any rational world, if I hired this person for this role, I'd get fired and then sued for negligence" way.)

You might get dozens or even hundreds of applications, but will any of them be worth the bytes their resumes are stored on?

Nope.

This little thought experiment is here to prove something simple: for all the work you do and the money you spend, you can't choose quality candidates to apply until they've chosen you first. This requires having a reason to choose you.

But we generally offer rather paltry reasons to choose you. Benefits? They look like everyone else's. A DEI statement? Meaningless without examples that define the shape of your commitment. "Good Place to Work" badge on the career site? Anyone can pay for those.

Most candidate experiences between "awareness" and "application" look exactly the same. Even when companies are legitimately different somehow, they do a horrible job communicating that differentiated value.

Consequently, we live in the world of employer *blanding*. But that doesn't have to be a fatal diagnosis.

Instead of thinking about how to attract people, you should be thinking about how to create the desire for what you have to offer.

It seems weird to see the word "desire" in relation to recruiting, and that in itself is strange. Don't you want people to want to work at your company? Don't you want them to want what you have to offer? Don't you want them to want what you offer so much that they ignore recruiters from other companies? Isn't that what your hiring managers, your HRBPs, and your leaders want?

So let's embrace the word "desire" because it rather accurately describes the core of employer branding and recruiting success.

Why this works

We all need jobs. It's expensive to exist in the world, so those of us not blessed with trust funds must work to do things like eat and watch Netflix.

But just because we are forced to get jobs doesn't mean we aren't all seeking to maximize our options. Maybe we'd prefer to work in an office than in a mine. Or prefer to work from home than in an office. We all have preferences of what we want in the place where we spend 8-12 hours a day.

But the word "preference" doesn't really do it justice. Think back to when you were a child. Did you want to be a recruiter? A brander? A marketer? Or did you want to be a fireman, a teacher or a baseball player? (My daughter is still planning on being a ballerina veterinarian who spends her weekends as a scientist on the space station. I'd make fun of her, but some part of me is still holding out hope that I hear back from that "emperor" role I applied for when I was 12.)

Any marketer will tell you it is a lot easier to sell your wares when people want them, when those wares align with customer values and allow them to do something they want to do. Jobs are no different. Between the choice of a job they will tolerate and a job they desire, there's no choice at all.

Where this falls apart

Desire is specific, which means it is also non-universal. For every person who thinks a Hemsworth or a Rihanna (or whoever is on this year's list of "most attractive celebrities") is the most attractive person in the world, there are dozens who prefer Alan Rickman and John C. Reilly or Megan Mullaly and Kristen Schaal.

It takes all kinds, right?

But that's the thing. You can't be desirable to everyone, so you need to be specific about whom you are desirable and why. That decision means there will be people who don't desire you and that's okay. In fact, that's likely proof that you're on the right track.

This unwillingness to be specific is the root cause of employer blanding. Leadership thinks of what employer branding does as the company mascot, hands them pom poms, and expects them to spout nothing but raw positivity.

> Go team! Go team!
> Who do we mean?
> We'll say it loud,
> Because we're proud!

This is about as specific as most companies get.

So if you want to create desire, you have to start by understanding what people will desire about you, which means getting specific (an idea we're going to dive into in a few laws).

Example

I have yet to see any proof that Google spends any real money on employer branding. And yet, they have topped Universum's "Most Desired Employers" list for over a decade.

Why?

Because in their early days, they found ways to be desirable among the "code all night" set in the Bay Area: Offer food, places to crash, snacks and coffee, all at a time when many coders still wore ties to work. They were seen as the best of both worlds: start-up credibility and freedom, but the stability and growth of a far more established company.

That feeling helped them attract so many applicants, that (according to rumor) Google often ignored the raw tonnage of applicants in theATS and only looked at candidates who were referred by someone internal.

That's the power of desire. Get it right, make it real, and you'll never want for quality applicants again.

Law #7: The Law of Quality

Quality beats quantity (and everything you're using now is probably focused on the wrong one)

This isn't my favorite law, but if I could only teach one law, this would be it.

And honestly, I remain stunned by how many people want to tell me this law isn't correct.

In a nutshell, employer branding differs from consumer and corporate branding in one significant way: The rest of the marketing and branding world wants more. More views. More leads. More impressions. More channels. More eyeballs. More shelf space. More share of wallet. More brand recognition. More subscribers. More views. More audience. More more more.

Employer branding doesn't want more. It wants better. Specifically, it wants better candidates and better hires. That is its remit.

It is a game of quantity versus quality. And employer branders only succeed when they focus on quality.

This claim may seem surprising at first, but once you stop and think about it, it should be clear as day.

The reason we don't often think this way is that we often take our cues and approach from consumer marketing. We play a strange game of "follow the leader." They care about programmatic, so we care about programmatic. They care about Tik Tok, so we care about Tik Tok. They care about Facebook Ads, so we care about Facebook ads.

We rarely stop to consider that their goals and our goals might be different. Because they are.

For a marketer, every dollar brought in is a good dollar. For a recruiter, not every application brought in is a good application.

Instead, we end up adopting their metrics (impressions, clicks, conversion, etc) despite the fact that those metrics aren't what we care about.

And since the employer brand industry is relatively small compared to consumer marketing, vendors and platform owners aren't going to scrap what works for 99% of their clients just to satisfy us.

We can't even turn to consumer branding for help. They are too busy fighting their own fight over metrics and purpose to offer much support. And ultimately, they think about quality in terms of finding the "correct" audiences of people who will likely consider their products in the future, which is a far cry from the level of quality we are focused on

Thus, we get herded like sheep into thinking about quantity when what we should be focused on (because it services recruiting and the recruiting process) is quality.

Why this works

This is basic math. If I have a hundred donuts to sell, the faster I can sell those donuts, the sooner I can get to making more, meaning the sooner I can sell out of my donuts, the more money I will likely make over the course of a year because I am spending more time making donuts than marketing and selling them. As a good little capitalist, I want to sell the maximum number of donuts and maximize my return, so selling more and faster is the win.

But recruiting doesn't operate by those rules. For every requisition you have, chances are, only one person can fill it. Let's say you're hiring a new director of sales. Are you going to hire the first person who applies? Or the first person who meets core requirements?

Of course not. You wait a week or four and sort the people who applied. There is a huge value to the business in getting great people "in seat" as soon as possible, but that's not how recruiting works.

It's not recruiting's fault. Every recruiter has dozens of stories of showing the hiring manager the perfect candidate a few days after the job gets posted, only to hear the hiring manager say, "Yes, that's great, but let's see who else applies."

Everyone in the process is attempting to maximize the quality of the candidate.

Where this falls apart

Non-employer branders hate this law. They reject the optics of focusing on quantity instead of quality as if their work was somehow inferior. But it isn't. Their job is to increase sales by finding more people who will buy.

Here's proof: Marketers don't talk about how they got the best lead. They talk about getting the most leads from a campaign. They don't talk about how this work will get the best view, but how it will get the most views.

Their only argument is that they care about quality in the shape of a "marketing (or sales) qualified lead" and that's true. There is a threshold of quality leads must make to be seen as useful, but then they want as many of them it can find. It is still a game of quantity for them.

Flip it around: are recruiters and employer branders rewarded for finding one amazing candidate or ten? Talent is a relative thing: if you brought in ten perfect hires, the hiring manager would hire "the best one" and generally consider the rest "rejects." Collecting ten perfect candidates instead of one or two provides almost no extra value.

Examples

You can see great examples of employer branding ignoring this law everywhere. They are always the brands without much of a point of view, the brands that epitomize "employer blanding" by trying to speak to everyone, trying to make the universe see them positively.

As we'll see in the next law, employer brand isn't served by being generically attractive. It needs to be attractive to someone specific, and broad pronouncements about how this is where you can do great work without defining what the work is, who the person is who will do great work or why this place isn't like other places with similar statements.

Law #8: The Law of Fit

Company, Job, Role, Person

The classic model of recruiting is pretty straightforward: post the job in as many places as possible and see who applies. This might be augmented with some sourcing, where you try to promote the job to potential candidates who seem to have the background the hiring manager is looking for.

It's an approach commonly seen in fishing, where you drag a net through the ocean and see what you get. Sure, you grab some tuna, but you're also capturing octopus, dolphins, rocks and things that aren't just useless, but cost you money to manage around.

Trawling the seafloor only makes sense when you think that every nurse is pretty much the same. That every salesperson is roughly equally effective. That every leader exists within a fairly well-defined band. You can lose a nurse and grab a new nurse's resume from the pile and go about your day.

And when jobs are all about following rules and meeting specifications, that kind of "commoditized talent" makes sense. You wouldn't search through a bag of nails to get the "best" one, would you? When each one is roughly like another, why bother hunting too hard for something better?

Sadly, that's not how businesses work anymore. The variance of value is incredibly wide (look at the difference between your best and worst salesperson: in many cases, the difference is measured less in degrees but in orders of magnitude) because jobs aren't about connecting dots as they are about finding new dots to connect and new ways to connect them. Jobs are more creative, and more complex (especially since anything that could get automated or shipped overseas already has been), requiring people who are willing to take their experience and apply it to a brand-new situation.

Despite more than a decade of begging Talent Acquisition teams to reject "post-and-pray" recruiting models that made sense 40 years ago, it remains the core of how most companies hire.

But "talent" (and that's a flexible word if ever there was one) is only half of the picture. Do you think Jony Ives would have become the designer of his generation if he worked at Caterpillar? Nothing against CAT, but their appetite for compelling design isn't the same as Apple's.

And I get that that's a bad example. Frankly, all examples that involve Apple are almost outliers.

Let's use a sports metaphor: If you're the greatest wide receiver in football, how much better would you look if you were paired up with an amazing quarterback who loved to throw it to you? Imagine how much worse your numbers would be with a quarterback who wasn't as good at passing more than 10 yards.

Or think about yourself. Think about the best job you ever had. Was it the best job because you were amazing? Maybe partly. But were you in a team that supported you the way you liked to be supported? Were you expected to deliver things you could excel at? Were you at a company that valued what you did?

Didn't having those things make you perform better? Didn't they make you happier at work?

If that job didn't hire you, but instead hired someone equally skilled but who worked in a different way, who delivered work at a different cadence, who preferred to make blog posts instead of social content, would they be equally happy?

Success at work is a function of the fit between the person, the role, and the company.

And employer branding is a major part of making that fit happen.

Why this works

Good hiring isn't about getting more applications (Law of Quality), but about finding the overlap between company, role and person. Once you see that you can't treat quality of hire like a commodity, something that can be swapped interchangeably like a screw or a light bulb with equal results, it becomes clear that we may have over-indexed on "finding the right person" while all but ignoring the thinking needed to define the role and the company.

Ahhh.. but you may be thinking to yourself: What do you mean? We have job descriptions and postings to define the role, and we have the career site and marketing to define the company.

But do they, though? What percentage of job postings are stolen from other job postings or even other companies? How can you describe the role using language designed for other roles at other places? And the answer is: you aren't.

So we aren't describing the job. Okay. Are we describing the company?

Not really. Very very very few companies have a meaningfully distinct brand. What's the difference between AstraZeneca and AbbVie? If you look at their career sites... not much. What about the difference between PwC and KPMG? Again, you'd need a microscope and years of experience in the industry to find daylight between them.

Over-indexing on the candidate is a natural extension of the company having all the power in a hiring relationship. Before 2015, the company that had the job on offer had way more power in the relationship than the candidate. It didn't matter what the difference between KPMG and PwC was because it's not like the candidate was getting offers from each and trying to weigh their options.

This is why employer branding is necessary to not only fill the gap, but provide the perspective that makes this real.

You might do a great job listing bullets to accurately describe the job (and let's be clear: employer branding has a lot to offer the job posting creation process), but the employer branding describes the company, providing the context for all those bullets. While job posts are meant to deliver some kind of value to the candidate even when stripped of all formatting and shared at a third location (e.g. job board), the employer brand shapes the perception.

The textually identical job posting from Twitter is NOT the same as the job posting from Moderna. The brand matters.

Without the brand, you're just a restaurant with a sign that says "WE HAVE FOOD!" and wondering why no one is ordering anything.

Where this falls apart

Yes, there are plenty of places where commoditized talent isn't just the norm, but is in fact, preferable. Look at McDonald's. Every burger, from hoof to burp, is run through a rigorous process, from ensuring cows have proper medication, to testing grind size and fat content, to equipping restaurants with that apply the exact right amount of mustard or mayo on a burger, to a centralized point of sale system. All of which ensures that while it is very hard to mess a burger up, there's not much chance for a single person to add their stamp on things, to make the burger better.

In places like these (and please excuse the use of a "burger flipper" as my example here), talent is truly commoditized and the employer brand has less of an impact.

Examples

Two years ago, it came out that junior Goldman Sachs analysts were working 100-hour work weeks. At the time, it seemed like a PR nightmare, that no one would ever want to work at this place that normally has hundreds, if not thousands, of applications per opening.

And at almost any other company, that would likely be true.

Why wasn't it true at Goldman Sachs? Why did a well-shared story like that not decimate their recruiting? Because every single person who applied knew full well that that was what was expected of them.

Goldman Sachs is not a place for feet-on-the-desk daydreaming or taking a it's-my-birthday-so-I-came-in-late break. It is a place where you push yourself like you've never pushed yourself before. You don't join GS because of their mission or discussions of work/life balance. You join because you know that if you work your butt off, there is a pile of gold at the end of this rainbow.

You don't join GS to learn. Or to meet people. Or to feel supported. Or because it has some clear social good.

You work there because the value transaction with the company is crystal clear: you give us the whole of your twenties and much of your thirties and in return we'll make you rich.

It's not just about what the company wants. About 8 years ago, GS launched an app to help people prepare to apply. Not interview, to *apply*. They created checklists and processes that ensured that anyone who applied knew full well what they were getting into. The definition about the expectations of the role and the working culture were spelled out in ways that your usual "a paragraph of boilerplate from legal and 17 bullets that look generic" job posting can't begin to match.

They did everything they could to ensure that the company and the role were clear. It was up to the candidate to decide if that's the kind of thing they wanted.

They were doing their part to create a fit.

(And if it matters, anecdotally, I have heard that GS has had no problems attracting people who want to work there despite the article.)

Law #9: The Law of Clarity

Specific, Attractive, Different and Real

Take a moment and think about all the information being sent or shared between the company and the candidate during any candidate experience (or is it "candidate's experience?" Have we gotten to the point where CX is its own thing?)

From the company side, you've got the career site, the job posting, years of LinkedIn posts, short videos (new and old), recent press releases from the company, what the recruiter says, what the interviewer says, and what the offer letter says.

From the candidate's side, you've got the application/resume, the LinkedIn profile, social media and thought leadership content, what gets said in the screening call, and what gets said at the interview. Perhaps your process includes a case study or a working sample.

Now let's get real here. Everything in the above list is deeply biased (at best), overly aspirational spin, or outright bullshit (at worst). Career sites make each company sound like they invented paid time off. Job postings are so filled with junk, you need a map and a native guide to try and interpret what the job even is. Social media channels are rife with "we took the day off to paint a school!" posts ignoring 99.9996% of what the company really does.

Oh, don't get all high and mighty, friend-o. Your resume is a set of cherry-picked wins glazed like a donut with "power words" and over-generous and poorly-attributed outcomes. And your LinkedIn channel is like if your resume came to life. Either way, none of them are really you.

Because of that, much of what both sides see and hear up to the interview is like looking at someone through their press clippings. Like trying to see what someone looks like in amazing lighting while the lens is smeared with Vaseline.

All this is to say that in the process of recruiting, there is a LOT of information flowing back and forth, but how much of it is useful?

On both sides, what everyone is desperately missing is clarity.

Now, clarity is... messy. What your lawyers think is clear can feel like trying to find a light switch in the dark while wearing sunglasses to you and me. What your hiring manager (an expert in their chosen field) thinks is clear is like trying to read hieroglyphics upside down.

So how can we decide what is clear?

Things that are clear meet four simple criteria: Specific, attractive, different, and real.

"Specific" meaning that what is said isn't bluster or spin, but concrete claims with proof. It's the difference between saying "we offer world-class benefits" and "we offer 12 vacation days, 21 PTO days, and pay 90% of all health insurance premiums." One is a nice thing to say, the other gives information.

"Attractive" meaning that it is something that the specific audience cares about and wants. Does your audience care that your CFO is speaking at a conference? Or that your CHRO won an award? If it isn't, then explain why your social channels are filled with content like that?

"Different" meaning things that show how your company is different from others. You've got a "fantastic place to work" award? So do all your competitors. You fill your social channels saying you care about LGBTQ+ people in June. How is that different than other companies? That line where you've got a great culture on your career site sounds a lot like the line on their websites saying the same thing. If your content isn't helping a candidate make an informed decision, it isn't clear.

Finally, is what you're saying "real?" Or is it a product of marketing copywriting to imply something that isn't there? Or is it what your CEO wishes the company were like? Or is it what people tell themselves when they choose to not look for a new job.

If you aren't SADR, you simply aren't being clear to your candidates.

And that's all they're looking for.

Why this works

We can't state the stakes highly enough. Aside from buying a house, selecting your next job is the most meaningful business decision most of us will ever make. Changing a job is changing a life. We need credible and meaningful information with which to make an informed decision.

Actually, the comparison to buying a house is surprisingly useful. When you search for a house, the average house listing is chock full of information. From how old the house is, how big it is, the school district it exists in, what the taxes were last year, photos of the interior and exterior, video walk-throughs, asking price, HOA situation, what it sold for last time and when, etc etc. No matter where that listing exists, it is deep.

Compare that to the amount of information you find on a job posting. While it may look like a lot of stuff, what is the salary? Who had that job last? Who is the manager? What does the office/cubicle/desk space look like? When was the last time you had to hire for this role? Did that person quit, get promoted, or get fired? What should you expect your insurance costs to look like? What is the AC set at? What is the complete WFH policy? Are you an Outlook company or a Gmail company? Or is it all Slack or Teams? Zoom or WebEx?

Looking at any job, you could easily come up with dozens of valid, useful and meaningful pieces of information that the company probably has at its fingertips that it chooses to NOT include. These include all the companies who talk about how much they care about (and spend on) the candidate experience. I presume their goal is to treat the candidates like mushrooms: keep them in the dark and feed them crap.

So set your company apart and get specific, attractive, different, and real.

The SADR model is designed to create clarity, the kind of clarity that leads to trust over time. And if you ask any recruiter, a candidate who trusts you is way more valuable than one who doesn't.

Where this falls apart

Most candidates are operating in a vacuum of information.

So give them some. Give them as much as you can.

This is the moment where someone from your legal or HR team would like to have a word with you. At this stage, you'll hear phrases like "material information" or "constitutes a promise." Now, for me, most words out of your legal team's mouth are advice. They are there to tell you where the risk is, should you pursue that path. Sure, what they say often sounds like a rule or a demand, but very often, it's just how they've been trained to communicate.

"Material information" is information that is not yet public which might impact the perception of the company and impact the stock price. Once you share material information, go ahead and immediately get yourself a lawyer because you're about to spend a LOT of time getting sued by lots of people.

"Constitutes a promise" means that what sounds like "a reason to engage" to you, sounds like a contract to someone else. And when you make a promise in your marketing, people will start calling your legal team and they will no longer be your friends.

Honestly, it doesn't take much water to make someone dying of thirst feel better. So while you might not be able to show pictures of the office or say the salary (yet), anything you can share that your competitors don't will serve you.

Examples

Clarity exists in many forms in many places.

If I were to look at your job application process, I'm probably going to be faced with a form requesting my demographics. That form is likely one of the worst-written things on your entire career site.

First, it's not necessary for a candidate to fill out that form and be a successful candidate. The data itself is voluntary in almost all cases. But it is written as being a mandatory part of the application.

Second, while there's a ton of verbiage about how the government mandates the collection of this data and that it isn't directly connected to employment, it sounds like it was written by the person who wrote the "do not remove this tag under penalty of law" tag on your mattress:

Semi-intentionally unclear about who should abide by these rules, or who the rule is meant to help.

The outcome is likely... rough. Underserved audiences might see the form as a means to filter out "certain types" of people and refuse to give it out of fear of being one of those people. Other audiences will assume the data will be used to support quotas of underserved folks, and refuse to give data for fear that they will also be filtered out because of it. The current language doesn't have the clarity of purpose to inspire trust, so consequently, you have a pretty dismal completion rate.

Go ask your HR team. You'll be surprised by what they tell you. I'll wait.

What if you replaced your legalese with something like, "[XYZ company] cares about doing everything it can to provide an open and inclusive workplace, and one of the ways we measure our success is by measuring basic demographic data. We can't get better if we don't know where we stand, right? So we are asking you to fill out the following form with your demographic information. If you choose to voluntarily complete this form, it will be immediately separated from your application and not be used in any way to determine who we select to call and interview. Thanks so much!"? Isn't that way more understandable and clear than what you have now?

Run it by Legal (they might ask that your language be used above their legal copy) and see the percentage of people who complete the form rise immediately.

Clarity works.

Law #10: The Law of Subjectivity

The best brand claims are subjective, which means you need to work ten times harder to validate them

Looking at the hiring process as, say, an alien would, you might wonder how a company can ever hire anyone.

For example: After interviewing with a company that it's likely you never heard of the day before you applied (statistically speaking), you get an offer. Then you quit your current role. But that "offer" isn't a contract. It's a... non-binding promise? An intention? Plenty of people have had their offer "rescinded" after quitting their current job.

If it weren't for the imperative to feed and house ourselves and our families, prospects would have rejected the whole thing long ago.

Recent news stories about fake companies hiring people, and getting a few weeks of work out of them before it becomes clear that the "employee" has been scammed only make this issue more clear.

Even in situations where everyone is trying their best to be upstanding and forthright, there's so much biased language, spin, agendas, misdirection, and bullshit that hours of talking can go by without much being said.

And what needs to be said in a more clear and direct fashion is why someone would choose this company. Your company. **What is the value you offer candidates to become employees?**

That sounds simple, but it really isn't. There are two kinds of value that an employer offers an employee: Objective value and subjective value.

Objective values are things that, when offered, all parties have a shared understanding of what's being offered. When the company offers a salary of $80,000, it's not $75,000. Or $80,000 Canadian dollars. There's no equivocation. It's a fact. Everyone knows what $80,000 means.

Other objective values offered would include the title, the start date, the office location, and specific benefits. Some roles come with stock or specific bonus structures. Defined paid time off. These are all things that are objectively true.

Subjective values are the things that you "offer" but it's not strictly clear that what you said and what they heard are the same. When you say that you offer "world-class benefits," what does that mean? Is dental included? Is it a 100% paid premium? What's the copay? What's the deductible? Will you pay for my gym membership? What if my gym is an MMA gym? Do you offer pet insurance? Are in vitro services offered? What about freezing eggs? What sounds like a "nice claim" is actually... nothing much at all.

Now, I don't mean to impune companies. I'll assume, for the sake of argument, that most companies aren't trying to obfuscate things. They are mostly trying to "sell" them. They are taking the same approach your grocery store does to a box of crackers. Have you ever looked at some of the "throwaway" language on store-brand food? It's hilarious. You'd think they had to split the atom to make those pretzels or that eating those nuts would lead to world peace.

But jobs aren't something you can sell. They are too important for flourishy language like that. Jobs demand specificity.

Especially when what you're talking about is subjective.

Because it turns out that what candidates want is the subjective stuff in a job: innovation, a mission, support from their team, a boss who wants them to grow, recognition, etc. But since you talk about those subjective ideas like they are fun things to claim and not the real reason someone's interested in the role, it isn't helping you.

Why this works

Way back when, we didn't know what a "reasonable" salary for a given job was. Were we being paid the market rate or were we being underpaid?

That seems like a long time ago. Even if we ignore full pay transparency laws, there's just too much data out there to not know what a nurse in Utah generally makes, or what a sales manager in a regional HVAC distributor generally makes.

While all parties have their guard up when they negotiate salaries, no one is rationally expecting people to work way below the norm. In fact, seeing a role where the pay is well above the norm may sound alarm bells.

So when you know that most inbound sales managers in your geography make the same amount of money, the only thing left that will influence their choice is... well, everything else. Once you're paid fairly, what do you want most? More professional development so you can make more money or have more impact down the road? Less oversight and supervision? More support from your team and company? A mission you believe in?

In a way, the internet and all its data has allowed us to focus more clearly and strongly on things beyond money.

Where this falls apart

On one hand, if you aren't offering people a salary and benefits within a normalized range, offering them a mission may not do much good. Subjective value only has value when base objective needs are met first.

And there is and will probably always be an audience of people whose primary (and secondary) focus is to maximize their objective value. The highest possible salary, the best title, the most perks, etc.

Those people tend to congregate in companies and industries where they can make that happen. Sometimes it is classically well-paid industries like trading and hedge funds, and sometimes it chases trends (enrollment data in comp sci courses spikes pretty hard once it becomes clear that there will be loads of very high-paying jobs in software development once Facebook and Google make real splashes).

You might lament the fact that you can't pay people as much as "those companies" but the truth is, you probably didn't want to hire the folks who are primarily motivated by money. Even if you did hire them, they would have left for a nickel more somewhere else.

Examples

There are some pretty smart and capable people who work in your university library. And in non-profits. And as teachers in a public school system.

They aren't confused, wondering why they aren't paid what blockchain special was making in 2019. They know the role they picked. They know that it wouldn't take too much to change roles and companies to make a lot more money, sometimes in roles or companies with less stress.

And if the objective value of money was their core motivation, they would.

But they don't. Maybe they want to give back. Or support others. Or be in an organization that rewards long-term thinking.

They are driven by a return on investment that isn't financial in nature. They have a different set of metrics by which to measure their choices.

And isn't the opportunity to make our own choices what drives personal satisfaction?

Law #11: The Law of Localization

A brand must be converted from abstract idea to something a target audience will recognize and resonate with

Let's wave our magic wand (what, do you not have one? That's unfortunate) and *poof* we have an employer brand. Whether it is an EVP, a brand promise, a brand direction, or some other variant or shape of a "brand," it now exists. Just check your deck. There it is. Yay!

So is everything better? Are your recruiters attracting more of the people they want? Is your career site supporting more compelling job postings? Do people in every appropriate field now think of you as an interesting employer?

Probably not. I mean, it's still just a slide on a deck. Maybe 20-30 words. It isn't a spell. It isn't magic (I'll take that magic wand back now).

Remember what the brand is trying to do: connect people to companies and roles that will serve them. All too often, we think of a brand as a "company-sized" thing. And while it starts that way, being company-sized only solves part of the problem: It might attract people to the company but ignores the more local issues of how it helps set expectations around what the role will offer.

As a concept, a brand is too broad to be useful. So in order to begin to extract its value, we have to put it through the process of localizing it to various audiences.

There is a pro and con to this level of abstraction. The nice thing is that as an abstract concept, anyone can look at it and see what they *want* to see in it. The bad thing is that when everyone sees whatever they want to see in it, it eliminates any value of alignment. Having been told what the elephant looks like, the blind men are free to think of the elephant as whatever they are touching.

Localizing takes the various ideas within a brand and decides which makes the most sense for that audience, translating those ideas into their language while preserving some sense of the central idea.

So if you have an EVP with four pillars (a relatively common situation), the brand-and-pillar-one might best apply to nurses, and the brand-plus-pillar-two would attract more of the doctors you want.

Here, the overall brand serves as a kind of anchor to all candidates, allowing the pillar (or pillars) to connect that anchor to that person. This is being specific to your audience's motivations while still creating alignment with the larger brand idea.

But the last step is to wrap those ideas in language. Once we know which parts of the brand we want to communicate, we translate those ideas into the local language.

Let's say you have an innovation message to share. To developers, you might talk about the amazing tools and tech they will have access to and the expectation that they will be expected to push themselves and create something new. To the salesperson, that message might be about how you have an innovative product to sell or that you're comfortable with innovative approaches to generating leads. To the QA team, that message might be that the QA team is completely integrated into the development process and doesn't exist as the "last step in delivery." To a recruiter, that message might be that this company has invested in employer branding and the training to make that brand useful. Same ideas, expressed in different ways to different audiences.

Every company needs to localize its brand differently. At a massive multinational company, the idea of localization will often involve culture and language. How you express innovation to the team in Chicago will be different than how you express it to the team in Copenhagen and Chennai.

But this is where the brand's abstract nature becomes a positive. Because I am translating "innovation" (the idea) rather than "innovation" (the word), I am allowing local teams to consider the idea and interpret and express it to their own audiences.

Why this works

Brands are conceptual. They exist as perceptions in other peoples' heads (see: The Law of Perception).

As things that exist exclusively in people's heads, they are exceedingly hard to convey accurately. Not to turn this into a semiotics lesson, but how do you know the color I see as "blue" is the same color or shade that you see as "blue?" Even if I were to say, "it's a soft blue that leans towards gray," we're almost certainly not thinking of the same color.

The way you break out of that trap is to reference local knowns. So instead of saying "blue" or "a light blue with some gray" you say, "the color of our scrubs" or "the color of the GE logo" or "Hex #3b73b9." You describe an abstract concept in terms that the listener will understand.

The same is true for your employer brand. When you say, "We're supportive!" that means... nothing. Support is a deeply abstract concept that everyone will consider and expect in wildly differing terms. Does "We're supportive!" mean, "four-day work week"? Or "We'll pay for your pet insurance"? Or "Once a month, we'll say, 'thank you' by buying the team some pizza"? All those ideas can accurately describe the idea of being supportive, but I bet your company leans close to one version of the truth or the other.

Localization is the act of taking that concept and making it more real, of describing the shape and attitude of the brand, making it less abstract and more concrete so that everyone has a shared understanding of what you're both talking about.

Where this falls apart

When companies "buy" a brand (hire an agency or consultant to uncover and/or research the company and working experience to craft a brand deliverable), the cost of "developing" it tends to lead to an under-spend on the localization. But localization is the middle layer that connects the abstract to the meaningful. It takes "We're changing the world!" and described it to a specific way in a language they will absorb and respond to

Many companies want to jump to the activation process because it's "cool" or "fun" or "what the kids are doing." (No, no one's ever said that last one.) And when they skip this step, they end up with pretty, flowery and aspirational claims that are flimsy at best (and feel like BS at worst).

But localization is also the process of translating the brand ideas into other cultures and languages. And here, there is an opportunity for failure. If you need to translate the brand idea of "innovation" into Tamil for the Chennai team keeping an eye out to express innovation as someone in that region of India might appreciate it, how will you know they haven't deviated too far? You'll need to actually re-translate it back into your language and test the ideas. Assuming a simple translation (or worse, running it through Google Translate) is begging for misunderstanding in an area that is both public and painful.

Examples

When you look at consumer descriptions of localization strategies, what you'll find is all about cultural and language localization. But for employer brands, it's more common to think of localization in terms of functional areas. Let's assume your brand is "Bright Future Made By You" (This isn't public information, so while this is an actual employer brand, I can't say who's brand it is).

If you tell a marketer "Join us, because this company is building a bright future made by you," what do you think they will think? Probably that you're full of crap. But if you run the idea in the brand through a localization process, you might consider that a marketer might be very interested to see that their work is driving and growing the company. This might suggest a company that is willing to listen to ideas from lots of different places under the guise that the best idea wins.

Suddenly, "bright future made by you" turns into, "Hey, look, as a marketer, I bet you have loads of good ideas that aren't being considered because you're not the boss. Is that a fair guess? Mmmhmmm... Yeah, I thought so. So I bet you'd be interested in working at a place that was marketing driven, but via hierarchy, but via merit. A place where the best idea was probably going to win. Does that sound interesting?" It's the same concept, but now it is connected to what a marketer cares about and might be looking for.

Law #12: The Law of Activation

A brand is worthless without perpetual and unceasing tactics and campaigns to get people to see and consider the brand

Having localized your brand to concern itself with things you various target audiences care about, it's time to activate the brand: turning conceptual ideas into deliverables like campaigns, content, ads, internal talking points, interview questions, job posting language, review site response boilerplate, and everything in between.

In short, this is the stuff your company was thinking it was getting when it agreed to an employer branding project.

To them, everything up until this point has been an academic exercise; speaking to staff, interviewing leadership, running focus groups, completing competitive audits aren't useful. Where all that thinking leads is.

The purpose of activation is to bring your brand thinking into the cold light of day. To stop talking about it in the abstract, but in terms of the things candidates will see, read, and absorb. If you're trying to get strangers to think of your company as a place that takes care of its people, what will you show and tell them to change that perception? Not what will that material be about, but what will that material be?

This is hard, because when you work in the abstract, people can hear it described but have a completely different picture in their head than what you have. This is the point at which all abstractions fall away and everyone is looking at the ad, the web site, the video, the job posting or whatever at the same time, seeing the same thing.

There are two core jobs at this stage, and they happen roughly in order.

First, this is everyone's chance to consider and evaluate the new brand as it goes out the door. Is this what they really wanted to tell candidates? Saying you're dedicated to supporting your people is a fine brand promise, but now that you look at it in an ad, is it really creating a meaningful differentiation? This is both a question of position (is the brand we built the right brand?) and creative (did we express the brand the right way?).

Second, are you making good channel choices? You have a new brand and came up with a great headline that you love. It looks great on a website, but does it make sense as a job posting? Or a LinkedIn post? Or as a Tik Tok video? As you bring your brand out, you must consider the channel context when activating.

Activation isn't just essential because it turns the concept into creative that people can see and respond to, but because you can change the creative, you can change the activation as much as you want without diminishing the brand itself.

Think of activation as fashion: hemlines and lapels change shape every year but a person will always be a winter or a summer forever.

That means you should think of your activation as campaign-driven fashion. How can we express the brand in a word pre-covid? During lockdown? And in a world of hybrid work? How does your brand expression change when your business is growing vs a slow down? You can change these ideas and messaging without changing the central ideas of the brand itself.

Why this works

Looking back at the Coca Cola example and a brand of "happiness," you can't just have a commercial that says, "happiness!" You can't repeat the word "happiness" over and over again until people feel happy. If they did, we'd all be standing in front of Jeff Bezos' house saying, "give me a billion dollars!" over and over again until our bank accounts exploded.

So what do you do? You build "things" (ads, headlines, career site copy, videos, job postings, automated messages, outreach messages, social posts, etc) that make people think and feel a certain thing. And then you connect that idea and feeling to your brand.

People don't see the ideas you're expressing, they see the "things" and infer those ideas. That's how you get people to believe that you care about something: they can see you talking about it everywhere and infer that that's what matters to you.

Where this falls apart

This is the "rubber meets road" part of brand development. This is where things get real.

And there are two very simple ways to screw it all up.

Challenge one: Stakeholders

Let's assume that 90% of your stakeholders have a tenuous grasp on what a "brand" actually is. Many of them think a brand is a logo (see: The Law of Perception). So when you say you are delivering the brand, they may have surprising reactions to what you share.

They may say they don't like a line, or that they don't like the photo or a visualization. Heck, they might say they don't like that color (been there, I assure you).

This is why we do all the heavy lifting of defining what makes you different, the subjective values you offer, and localizing it to an audience. Because that line, image and color isn't for the stakeholders. It's there to deliver a message (the brand) to the target audiences. They may not like the line, but that line will deliver the right message to the right person.

When in doubt (or when in conflict), go back to the brand idea. Go back to the localization. Ask the objector, "Our only goal is to deliver [brand message] to [audience]. I understand that you have preferences, but my goal isn't to hire you. You already work here. My goal is to engage [audience] with the message that's specific to our company. Do you think this doesn't solve for that?"

Challenge two: Textualism

For fellow fans of the movie Inception, you might remember the idea that you can't tell someone an idea because if you do, it won't be absorbed. The idea needs to be created in someone's mind. That's why I can't say, "you should just be happy" and expect you to change your mood. People become happy (or sad or angry, etc) on their own.

But so much employer branding content is "We care about our people!" or "We're focused on innovation!" or "We're changing the world." They are saying "happy!" over and over again hoping that it makes people happy.

Good activation sparks an idea. Look at Coke. Maybe one out of ten ads use the word "happiness" which means nine out of ten ads are trying to spark a feeling of happiness without using the word. If you want to be known for innovation, it isn't enough to say it. You have to show it. You have to show the thinking behind it. You have to show failures and blind alleys that lead to insight and eventually innovative work. You don't have to say innovation to get someone to think it. In fact, you should avoid saying it at all.

You could distill Moby Dick into simply, "man vs nature and the poisonous nature of revenge." So is saying that the same as reading Moby Dick? If you read Moby Dick, won't you find far deeper meaning and connection to the book than if you just read the summary of its themes?

Examples

Pinterest's employer brand content is a great example here. If you look at their career site and social media, the word "empower" isn't posted everywhere. Instead, they talk about how they are supporting people as they start businesses. They talk about "ideas from anyone, made for everyone" and "gives organizations who are building innovative mental health solutions the resources to scale their impact and ensure long-term success."

They don't say the word "empower" much. They are working from an assumption that what they are doing is empowering and talk about that. It allows the reader to infer, make leaps on their own about what that brand cares about and offers.

Law #13: The Law of Options

There's always more than one way to achieve your goal

For a very (very) long time, Glassdoor told companies that it held a magic (and proprietary) formula about whether you had a "great" company to work for or not. It was a formula that resulted in a single number between 0 and 5, which we were told was how we rated as an employer.

I've been pitched a dozen different products in the last six or seven years who have tried to tell me, "This is how you solve your employer brand problem." Sometimes they were spamming/broadcasting tools, sometimes they were chatbots, sometimes they were reputation management tools, and sometimes they were video tools.

Look at the different skills "employer branders" bring to the table. Some are writers, some are videographers, some are narrative storytellers, some are visual designers, some are social media experts, some are ad builders, some are project managers, some are political creatures, and some are strategists.

What should all this tell you? That there are almost infinite paths toward making your employer brand create change.

Whatever your situation, whatever your goal, there is no one way to make your brand more useful.

You have lots and lots of options.

Do you want to get more people to know about you?

Buy some ads. Tell better stories. Get more of your staff to share content. Write a job posting so interesting, people share it organically. Build a clever video and edit it to look like a hotshot YouTube content creator made it. Better yet, make a parody of what a hotshot YouTube content creator would make and post it on YouTube. Then share it with them. Create an industry event and invite industry publications to cover it. Write an article revealing something about your industry most people don't know and pitch it to a reporter.

Do you want to change the way people who know you see you?

Find specific stories of how individuals have changed while working there and tell those stories (on social, in a video, on a blog post, in an outreach email). Define your mission to be less "woo woo" and more "achievable goal everyone has a hand in achieving" and build a campaign to share it more widely. Record an impromptu camera-phone video with the CEO about where the industry is heading and what makes your company suited for that future (don't worry, you're going to have to run it by comms and legal). Screengrab a Slack thread by leadership talking about how people should take care of themselves (see previous note about comms and legal). Work with fulfillment to put a note from the product lead (and signed by the product team, QA, and anyone who touched the product) into every deliverable thanking them for purchasing.

Do you want more people to want to work there?

Run a live virtual event where your product team talks about what they are building and the technology they use to build it. Write a series of social posts and get everyone on a team to commit to sharing, commenting, and engaging with the post to ensure the content becomes more credible over time. Make your hiring manager a social media rock star. Go spend $20 bucks and get all the cool-kid video effects and apply them like a drunken influencer. Create a video about an intern who was hired full-time that looks like a professional crew shot it. Sponsor anyone at your company who wants to run a local 5k and make sure they all have matching shirts. Go to an industry conference and live-tweet/thread the entire event (with an opinion).

Do you want to help people self-select out?

Tell a story about someone who on paper was a perfect hire and how the decision was made to not go forward and why. Give it a happy ending wherein the rejected person landed at a company better suited to them and you landed a better-fitting hire. Make the job posting shorter but more specific about what the job is intended to accomplish (rather than a list of skills). Instead of a "goofy" question when someone fills out the application, ask them, "If you could work at any company (and we didn't exist) where would you work and why?"

When it comes to making your brand more effective, there are always options.

Why this works

An employer brand is a perception of what it's like to work at a company based on dozens (if not hundreds or more) of interactions, touchpoints, and experiences. It is multidetermined, a system with so many permutations of inputs, there is no one lever you can use to create change.

Some levers won't work at all, and some give you exactly what you wanted. And there are others which might have ancillary benefits (maybe they're cheaper, easier, faster, give you a chance to engage new audiences, are a reason to talk to leadership about your work, aligns with what the marketing team is doing, etc).

Smart employer branders see the bigger picture. They understand that success isn't a straight line, and that selecting the obvious solution doesn't allow them to build relationships with other people, relationships that they will need to call on down the road.

Here's an example: At Groupon, I was trying to encourage more staff to complete the Google form that became the employee profile we were posting online. I knew there was a limitation on how many people would engage if I asked them to complete the profile.

Instead, I spent $100 on a limited run of stickers for people who completed the profile. As a tech company, everyone had plenty of stickers on their laptops, but they were all designed by the comms team, who had a very specific aesthetic. By designing something myself, I could build something obviously different, which made the stickers stand out. People who completed the profiles were thrilled to add stickers to their laptops, and when asked where they got it, would direct them to the Google form. Would it have been cheaper to ask people via email or Slack? Maybe. But by taking a different approach, I was making people who were willing to play my weird little game (before everyone knew about it) a little clout they could show off. That clout created more participants in teams I may never have realized existed.

If you have options, you need to make your choices more strategically.

Where this falls apart

Human nature. We all want there to be "right answers" to the work we do.

There are no right answers. Anywhere. There are layers of complexity, ambiguity, and confusion. No one knows the future.

But people want to be seen as rational. They want there to be a right answer in recruiting, hiring and marketing, places that are not rational. Not even close.

Human nature says that the size of the intervention is proportionate to the size of the effect. That we can only make smart decisions rationally. That two plus two is always four.

Employer branding is deeply irrational. It plays in emotions because that's what drives behavior. That's how you get people to take action and make choices.

Do this job for any length of time, and that becomes clear. But you'll be surrounded by people who think rationality is the only way.

You will need to show people that there are always options.

Examples

Let's say you send a box of cookies to every candidate you interview. That is a $25 charge per interview. That's no small potatoes to a company hiring 100-200 people a year.

A few things happen when you send everyone cookies.

One: If the hiring manager knows that there are real costs with interviewing another candidate, it might make them hesitate before looping in a third or fourth candidate into the pile of people to talk to. Hiring managers like to pretend wasting a candidate's time and an interview panel's time has no hard costs, but suddenly knowing there's a $25 charge with their name on it creates just enough extra consideration that they start to be more judicious about who they interview, which leads to faster hiring.

Two: No one will ever say, "I work here because they sent me some cookies once." That's crazy. On an individual level, cookies shouldn't make a difference. But if you look at your data, you'll find that cookies might result in a meaningful increase in the offer acceptance rates.

Cookies don't change minds. But they do validate claims a company might make about how well they take care of their people. Sure, a lower health insurance premium is great, but they aren't as tangible (and delicious) as cookies.

Does this mean that cookie delivery should be a central pillar of your talent strategy? Of course not. It could be, but it is only one way you can be reinforcing what makes your company the way it is.

Because you always have options.

Law #14: The Law of Customers

Employer branding isn't just about recruiting, but recruiting is always its first customer

Corporate branding has a lot of impacts, everything from helping to increase interest in investment to increasing interest in their products. But who is corporate branding's first customer? The company itself. That means focusing less on individual teams or products and focusing on making the company look attractive.

Consumer branding has a lot of impacts, everything from increasing the stock price to generating interest in working there. But consumer branding's first customer is the consumer. Their focus is first, second and always on generating new customers and keeping the customers they have,

So before I reveal the obvious third part of that idea, I feel the need to wade into the question of "where should employer branding live?"

Last time I checked, 55-60% of EB functions live in TA with 30-35% live in Marketing, and the rest in Comms.

There are some really good arguments for each. You can make a solid case that it requires a "marketing brain" to do good employer branding, that marketing tools are more useful to the EB owner. I get that. But I also buy the idea that living in TA means a closer relationship with recruiters and candidates, that ideas are more likely accepted if they come in the form that TA is used to. And there's a strong argument that employer branding is a kind of communication to and about employees, so it should live in comms (I will mentally put some asterisks next to comms based on personal experience, but I know my experience wasn't the norm).

Those arguments focus on function. For my money, because an employer brand is such a big job with a million ways to do it well (see: Law of Options), what matters is the person in the role. If its someone with marketing skills, they will do the most good in TA. It's the fastest way to level-up on recruiting thinking to ensure good work gets adopted. If they are a recruiter, they need to live in marketing to get a crash course in how marketing thinks and moves.

But in the end, what matters most is who the customer is. And in employer branding, while there are so many knock-on effects for the work being done, the first customer is always the candidate or future employee.

Sure, strong employer branding can increase morale. It can increase advocacy. It can create stronger connections between recruiters and their hiring managers. (See my ebook on the proof that EB works, straight from the EB managers' mouths.) https://diyemployerbrand.com/proof

But all that takes a back seat to one simple idea: Are you helping people understand who you are, what you offer, and how you're different so that they can make an informed decision about applying and accepting a role there?

All the good you're going to do for the company starts with that simple idea.

Law #15: The Law of Expansion

The recruiting funnel is bigger than you think

I'll admit it. I shoulder some of the burden for getting TA to think of hiring as a kind of funnel.

Ten years ago, "the funnel" was almost a mystical idea in recruiting, bringing order to chaos, turning the irrational and complex series of clicks and thinking of a prospect into a candidate and a new hire. It turned the myriad of paths people took to learn about you and apply and turned them into a straight-forward idea you could wrap your arms around.

There's a saying that's often credited to statistician George Box: "All models are wrong, but some models are useful." And in an industry that was expanding almost exponentially as the internet offered new channels and opportunities to engage people, where every day felt more chaotic than the last, the funnel was a very useful tool.

But the tool was designed to simplify and streamline, allowing us the chance to approach recruiting from an "internet mentality" instead of a "classified ads and phone calls" one.

In the ten years since I stood on a stage talking about the funnel, recruiting and talent acquisition has matured. The funnel, once a tool to allow us to manage the chaos, is now a kind of trap. It limits our thinking, telling us that the only people we need to consider are those looking for jobs and the only action we care about is getting a candidate to apply.

Employer brand is the answer to the question, "what's beyond the funnel?"

The funnel usually starts the moment a candidate takes some kind of action that tells you that they are looking. They visit a career site. They click an ad. They start searching on job boards. They engage with your posts on social media.

All of TA is focused on the moments between that and the acceptance or onboarding. Sourcers think about what kind of message it will take to get someone outside the funnel to enter it, but really, TA is the process of converting interest into intent and action.

And in a world where the company with the open role holds all the cards, having the job is enough. You're probably too young to remember, but there was a time when simply posting "Help wanted" was enough to get a pipeline of candidates.

Not so anymore.

Companies who succeed are those who think beyond the funnel. They aren't waiting for people to get interested, they are working to create interest. They are sending messages to people who likely won't look for a new job for months, or even years. They are looking beyond the funnel to create their own demand.

Great talent doesn't "search for jobs." They have a list of companies they already know something about and have an affinity for. A pre-established consideration set of companies they'd want to work for. For great talent, by the time they are thinking about looking for a new gig, it's too late.

Employer brand asks, "How do I get on that list?" "What would someone like that want to know that would make them interested in us enough to learn more?" and "Where should that information live so that it gets in front of them?"

Remember that 90-95% of people you would want to hire are not "in-market." They are not ready to read job postings or have a "casual chat" about their place in your organization. The tools at recruiters' disposal are not useful here. They are focused on getting the 5-10% of candidates in-market to convert and apply.

Employer branding thinks above the funnel and can reach that 90-95%

But it also thinks below the funnel, well past the offer acceptance or even day one. They think about what makes for a great long-term hire? A person who sticks around, gets promoted, creates something of value inside the company.

If your company hires 100 people, 50 will be gone in 18 months. Why did some stay and some leave? What stories should you be telling to shift hiring to the people who are more likely to stay? How can you set expectations at the beginning of their job search journey that will change how they see their job for the first year and beyond?

And how do you leverage the people who stick around? How do you get them to become advocates for the company?

When you are thinking about what value your employer brand can bring to the company, think about how you can expand the funnel.

Law #16: The Law of Relationships

Success in talent acquisition will come from relationships, not from treating recruiting like a transaction (more farming than hunting)

This list of laws was written in a very specific order. We start with some of the foundational ideas that help us understand what branding is (strategy, focus, perception, etc). Then we move to the laws that help us see branding in the light of hiring and talent strategy (desire, quality, fit, clarity, etc). Then we establish the laws that define the means of success (subjectivity, localization, options, etc).

Now we reach what I think of as "outcome" laws. These are the second-order effect laws that are only true because the previous laws are true.

The first of these outcome laws is the Law of Relationships.

There is a myth in modern work that great work happens via technology. That email would allow us to communicate fluidly across continents at speed, but what it really led to was the development of complete bodies of information to be trapped in other peoples' archived folders. That Slack would turn the text revolution on its head to create easily searchable async conversations going back to the foundation of the company, but what it did was turn our phones against us, creating low levels of PTSD in hearing that specific chime that a new message had arrived (to the point where years after being in a Slack org, the chime played on a Slack commercial immediately made me remember how much I disliked a specific boss),

Technology is great, but when you peel away the sales pitches and obvious salivation for a successful exit, it exists to create and support relationships. Tech may tell you that it is "making information transfer more fluid and more speedy, but it exists to make relationships work.

Because at work, assuming you aren't working a factory floor, relationships matter. Relationships are how complex and interesting work gets done.

If a job can be codified into clearly described steps and processes, someone has already figured out how to automate it with software, program a robot to do it, or shipped the work to the country with the lowest salaries. Everything else requires relationships.

But employer branding all too often focuses on tech. And tools. Or events (which is really just a tool in a physical space). They want to talk about how many people they reached instead of if they were worth reaching. They want to show off their creative instead of asking who is using it.

The Law of Relationships is here to remind us that the outputs, the tactics, the creative are all well and good, but the best employer branding happens because you build relationships.

Without relationships with recruiters, they won't listen to your advice and take advantage of your resources. And you won't get the front-line feedback you need.

Without relationships with staff, your advocacy plan won't get out of the gate, and your branding will need to rely on costly marketing channels. And you won't hear about interesting work being done in the company.

Without relationships with hiring managers, they will see your work as "more boxes to tick" as they hire instead of as extra resources they can use to hire better. And you won't have a network of people who will talk about how valuable your work is, or in-roads to staff whose stories you need to tell.

Without relationships with leadership, you won't have anyone who can support you as you make strange requests that further the brand (when all of HR and Legal freak their geek out because you're suggesting that giving rejected candidates actual useful interview feedback, you need a leader in your corner who can at least explain the value when you aren't in the room... because you're almost never in the room when the real conversation happens).

Relationships are the fuel, not only of your work but of your career. There are three ways an employer brander makes an impact.

First, by building great tactics. Branders start with a skill. Maybe they write well. Maybe they are ace social media managers. Maybe they can make videos. Maybe they can craft job postings. Whatever. The goal is to get good at one's craft, and maybe even add on others. But mastering your craft only gets you to the "how to write the perfect tweet" stage. It doesn't ask the question, "Why are we tweeting?"

Second is in managing strategy. That's how you answer the "why are we tweeting?" question. Along with the "Would this be better as a video or an internal comms channel campaign?" Strategy is how to maximize the resources you have to create the biggest impact. But it isn't as concerned with how to aggregate more resources.

Third is political. This is where you ask, "How can I get other teams to give me more resources so we can level up our work?" Then strategic assumes good results lead to more budget, but politics assumes resources already exist, it's just a matter of finding who would pay for what you can deliver.

As you progress up the ladder, you will use less tactical skill in favor of strategic skill, followed by seeing how you make an impact by playing the political game. As you move up, relationships matter more and more. In fact, relationships are how you move from one rung of the ladder to the next.

Law #17: The Law of Humanity

Employer brand is the most human-feeling part of any brand

Honestly, out of all the laws, this one may be the most controversial.

Sure, when I say that employer branding is the only kind of marketing that thinks in terms of quality over quantity, the marketers get all feisty. And when I say that the employer brand comes from all parts of the company, people try to turn it into a conversation about "where should employer brand live within the organization?" (For what it's worth, I am 1000% sick of that question. It's like a dog chasing its tail. Who cares what the answer is if the organization doesn't understand the value of employer branding and wants to get behind its success?!??!?!)

But when, as I did this week at RecFest (If you feel like you missed out, you're right. You should absolutely go next year), I say that employer branding is the human face of a company's brand, I expect employer branders to jump out of their seats and shout a la Braveheart. "Yes! We are playing a vital role in how the entire business is perceived by presenting and communicating the reasons people love to work there! A strong employer brand is the yin to consumer branding's product-focused yang and together, we build the company!!!!"

[Shouting ensues and then we charge down the hill to meet the enemy...]

Instead, I get a lot of blank stares. Not even nods or expressions of agreement, but more like I'm reciting arcane facts from Wikipedia that have no frame of reference. (Did you know there's a road that is both in Canada and the United States? It's called the Canusa Road...)

So let's close the gap, because when an employer brander is having a rough day, when they feel like their work amounts to polishing the INSIDES of the plumbing for all the value they are delivering, they need to remember that they are doing something amazing that impacts the entire company.

If you look at how most companies think about branding, it starts with the **product brand**: What is the product? What is its unique value proposition? What are the features and how do they solve a customer's problem? If you're selling SaaS, no one talks about who coded it or who tested the code. At best, you'll learn a little about the founder(s), who perhaps had a problem and built a tool to scratch their own itch. But there's nothing about the person who decided the next feature set or who built the marketing. To consumers, the product is a black box. It might as well have sprung fully-formed from Zeus' head.

When you're buying a product, the company wants you to buy it based on the value of the product, because if they can establish and prove that value, you'll keep buying it.

This is 100% of the branding when the company is small because the company has only one product. The product brand is the company brand.

But as the company grows, someone will be put in charge of the **corporate brand**. It might just be a function of showing how one company can have a shared perspective that connects multiple products serving multiple audiences. Think how the iPhone and the Macbook have different audiences and taglines, but in the end, they all share Apple's idea of how technology should look and feel.

That role may expand to include investor relations, when the investors aren't just two or three venture capital firms, but dozens of companies or even the entire investor market when you go public. The **investor brand** is the story the company tells about its long-term future. It illustrates how their specific take on the market and market trends will leave that company in the driver's seat at some point in the future, so start buying equity and stock now. And while CFOs will say all investors are not created equal (there is cache that comes along with Andreeson-Horowitz or Berkshire Hathaway's invest compared to when Mark's Big House O' Funding signs a check), in the end, the story they tell is the same: we are going to get much much bigger, so join now.

Note that the investor brand doesn't say much (if anything) about who works there and why. There's an assumption that every who joined is aligned to that vision of a bigger company and a great payday around the corner, but that kind of motivation is thin, especially when you're employee #1278.

There's a gap in the brand.

People.

And this is where the **employer brand** comes in. It isn't the sales pitch we make about why someone should join us. It is the expression of humanity to the market. How much, how little. What the people who work there care about and how much they are cared about and cared for.

Because as much as consumer branding talks about the product, who made the product? Who thought it up? Who tested it? You can't tell me that a product built by "just a bunch of faceless salary collectors" will be the same as one built by the team at Nike. Future product ideas and executions don't come down from God's fax machine, they come from the people who work there.

Which means your sense of a company's future isn't just based on a semi-famous CEO on the cover of a magazine, but the hundreds and thousands of people who push the idea further, who got the feedback and identified the insight, who made the product real.

And when leadership tenure keeps getting shorter (current CMO tenure is roughly 18 months), why should an investor "believe" in the leadership if they won't be around to see their dreams made real?

Employer branding is the voice of the people, the expression of the real, the path forward and differentiation from other firms.

And that is where we live.

Law #18: The Law of One Brand

There is only one brand. Your success will be determined by how well you connect to and support the larger brand

Here we are. The final law of employer branding. And this one is probably the biggest. Or the most obvious. Or maybe just the least understood?

In the last law, we talked about the consumer brand, the corporate brand, the investor brand and how that triumvirate creates a gap: the people who make the company happen. No people, no company, but those people aren't reflected in that brand structure.

That's where the employer brand fills the gap.

But in filling that gap, it allows the brand to stop being three or four separate sub-brands, but brings them together, coalesces them into a single brand. The company brand.

Because there is only one brand.

A company, when you peel back all the mythos and re-written history, exists to allow people together to do something they couldn't do alone. It is a structure and a series of agreements to ensure that everyone can contribute and be rewarded.

That's all.

A company is a collection of people with a common purpose and goals.

It may do many things. It may have people achieving different goals, but it is one company.

And that one company has a brand.

Your brand is a prism. You look through it to see and connect with prospects and candidates. Consumer marketers see through it to engage customers. Investor relations looks through it to talk to institutional investors and analysts. But it is still one prism that you all share. When you lift your side of it, it serves others.

So when the stock price goes up, you will find more people applying. When the product fails, you will see fewer people interested in responding to your outreach.

When you build stories of the people who work there, consumer and corporate marketing can use those stories to support more emotional connections with customers. Those stories speak of the internal working culture, which indicate the likelihood a company will thrive, which supports what the investor relations team is trying to instill.

It's all connected. It's one brand.

The brand is the extension of the company that lives in people's minds. When I think of Target, what do I think of? What do you think of? It is the products and the feels of the store, the service, the app, the boxes that sometimes show up and how they are (surprisingly poorly) packed. It is the person wearing red. It is the trucks on the road.

It's all one brand.

And as employer branders, we need to treat it as such.

Realistically, there are some challenges to face.

First, before employer branding came along to fill in the gap, the brand may have been managed by people in different departments. Marketing, obviously, but investor relations often reports to the CFO. The comms team can report to any number or execs, including the CEO.

It was the rare company who were structured to think in terms of "one brand" before we showed up.

Second, most employer branders would say that they feel disconnected from the "larger" brand. Even when they are assigned to the marketing team, they feel like they are on the outside looking in (and that's even more so true when they aren't on the marketing team). Their tools are different, their clients are different, and their goals are different. Their work doesn't naturally slot into the larger marketing picture, and marketers are often too busy to sit and think about how to use what you're building. That work is on you, but having to do it takes time and energy away from the work itself.

Third, thinking in terms of one brand is an ideal it takes time and work to achieve. It is an aspiration. Few companies are in that model. You have to have the cultural maturity to connect the different brand-associated teams, to potentially ask professionals to give up access to leadership in service of supporting a complete brand.

But just because it is heard doesn't mean you should ignore it.

When you talk about employer branding, stop talking about it as something *you* own. Or as something that will help recruiters. When you're talking about your work, plant seeds. Let people know that there is only one brand, and that you are merely one servant of it.

Employer branding has the power to make immediate impacts, but this is where you have to play the long game. It requires building networks and connections and relationships. It means working harder and creating the time to be in more of those meetings where different parts of the brand are discussed. It means serving the different holders of the brand what you have in packaging they understand and can immediately use.

It's hard work, but this is how you make your employer brand make the greatest impact on the company.

Conclusion

Once you understand the laws of physics, you can design houses, cars and rockets.

I hope that with this understanding of the laws of employer branding, you'll be able to build employer brands for any kind of company, regardless of whether you're in the talent acquisition team, the comms team, or the marketing team.

I firmly believe that employer branding can change recruiting and hiring for the better (I mean, NO ONE is a fan of the way it's done now), and I hope these laws allow you to find your own path forward.

-James

Also by James Ellis on Amazon

- *Talent Chooses You*
- *The Employer Branding Handbook*
- *Employer Branding for Small Business*

Printed in Great Britain
by Amazon

59036169R00056